IT'S ALWAYS BEEN YOU

IT'S ALWAYS BEEN YOU

Jabari Baxter

PALMETTO
PUBLISHING
Charleston, SC
www.PalmettoPublishing.com

Hardcover ISBN: 9798822958913
Paperback ISBN: 9798822958920
eBook ISBN: 9798822958937

TABLE OF CONTENTS

INTRODUCTION

Hi, my name is Jabari Baxter! I'm going to let you in a little secret. This is my third time erasing my intro. In fact, it is Thanksgiving Day for me as I am writing to you. I have been racking my brain wondering what I could say to you that would allow me to share a little piece of me. Well, this is the last time I'm going to erase my intro because I think the best way I can do so is to be transparent and say the things that we don't want to say. Have you ever wondered how you would know if you met "the one"? I know I have. I've been told that when you least expect it, he or she will come to you, but if you're like me, you have met a lot of people, but something does not seem right. It's not that you're being picky or that person doesn't meet your standards, even though that plays a part, but you do not feel that spark, that zip of lightning running through your heart that you see in the movies.

What if I told you that you can have that feeling? What if I told you that you can have that romantic love? What if I told you it would only be from the love of God that you can experience that supernatural, magnetic pull that you cannot describe?

August 29, 2021, at approximately 5:15 p.m. was the start of what I was yearning for in a woman. Here's what scares most of you, including myself. What if I might lose her or him? I'm afraid of losing that person because of my experiences. Trust me, I get it, I do, but through my growth with God, He has told me that this is not going to be the end. There is another life waiting for you in heaven, and it's going to surpass your wildest dreams. With that in mind, I have spoken to my love, a letter, a message. Call it what you will, but I know this is not the end. So, I share my heart with you to let you know and feel that it is not too late for you. Love is the only thing that matters in this life and the next, so why not?

I encourage you to write the initials of the love of your life. No one has to know or understand your heart. It will be just between you and God. This might be the shortest book you have ever read, but I pray this will encourage you to express your love to the one you love.

Love to

THE HEART SPEAKS THROUGH DREAMS

I had a dream about you. It felt so real. Why did I have to wake up? I want that dream; give back that dream. Why do my inner thoughts tease me? My outer thoughts want to focus on life. Is it because I have pictures of you on my fridge? Anyone with any sense would take down any memories that would hinder you from your focus. Well, maybe I don't want to focus on life because life sucks! I want to focus on things that are real and eternal (Philippians 4:8,).

Love to...

A MAGNETIC PULL THROUGH THE HEART

I was in the shower when I heard my front door open. I grabbed anything close for protection. When I opened my bathroom door, I saw you My heart dropped, and it was as if there was a magnetic pull that had us kissing, as if this was the very moment we've been waiting for. It took every fiber in my soul to push you away. I asked you "Babe do you see me in your future? If so, then we have to stop and honor God. If not, let's go to my bedroom right now and make this last forever, and then our lips shall never touch again." I wonder which answer you would choose.

Love to…

HEARTBEAT

I was sitting on the couch thinking. I heard a knock on the door; I looked at my phone and it was 11:58 p.m. I opened the door, and it was you! You said, "I'm sorry for showing up late. I don't really know why I am here." I placed my hand on your chest, then I grabbed your hand and placed it on mine. I said, "Do you feel that?" Both of our hearts were beating fast, not even a Ferrrari could match our speed. I drew in slowly, touched the side of your face, and we began to kiss. It's just as you see on television—everything began to close in, and we could literally feel the earth rotate. My soul did not want to push away, but I had to ask, "Do you see me in your future?" I do. I just hope that you do too.

Love to…

TRUE LOVE

Ten years have passed since you moved. I was working in my yard, and I heard someone say, "Jabari?" It was you! You said, "I'm sorry, are you Jabari?" I could sense the confusion. I was bulky, my facial hair had gotten thicker, and I now wore glasses; I responded, "The one and only." You came to say hi, wanted to know how I was doing and if I was seeing anyone. I told you that I wasn't, and by the look on your face, I could tell you was relieved and surprised. I returned the question back to you, and you said, "No!" You cried happily with tears of joy as you ran to kiss me. They say love needs to be worked on, but I say true love from God never dies. I wonder if you believe that to be true. Do you really know how much I love you?

Love to…

HEAR ME

My imagination runs deep, and even though it's just an imagination, it lights up the very inner being of how I feel about you. For those who are reading, if you are reading, just maybe you'll say you do as well.

Love to...

DESTINED

One day you will see my writing come to life and you will see my whole heart and soul touching yours. I used to tell you how I felt, but somehow, I don't think you thought it was real or eternal, that we were destined for each other. You don't see what I see in you, and that's okay. Truth be told, my love, you'll never be able to see what I see, but my God can! He will, just you wait, but please don't stop loving me. Our love is the only thing that is going to make us work. Be patient, and you'll see that we were meant to be.

Love to…

SING

I was going for my daily stroll in the park when I bumped into what appeared to be an outdoor gazebo. When I stepped inside, all I could think about was dressing it up and making it look so magical. Then I began to sing "Love" by Musiq Soulchild. I did that because you could literally hear your voice echo. My voice began to multiply as if I had my own backup singer. I bet if you were to sing in here, not even the heavens could deny your request. Maybe you'll never be able to find your way here, but by the grace of God that you so happen to sing, my love, sing!

Love to...

SOULMATE

One of my favorite television shows I watched when living on my own was *How I Met Your Mother*, one of the funniest shows you'll ever see. One of the reasons that I loved the show so much was because of one of the main characters, Ted. He was the narrator of the show, but he believed that his soulmate was out there waiting for him. So he would search and search by going on dates (more than I could ever go on) and came up empty-handed. Without giving you the whole outline of the show, Ted had a female best friend. Her name was Robin. All the viewers knew she was the mother and soulmate, but with every episode, they gave us a reason not to believe it was so, but not me, my love, I knew! Turns out, Robin was not the mother, but, in fact, the soulmate. You may not be my right now, but you're my forever.

Love to…

LET ME SERVE

I was at the gym, and I thought to myself, I don't really care about the results that I put into my training. I just want to feel good and healthy. Then, I thought, I wonder what you think about a fit man? Then I would have a secondary motivation to push myself even further. If you're reading this, you probably would say, "Don't do this for me. Be your own man. Do it because you want to. Don't let me change you." A genuine woman would say that, but not if they know me. In this life, all I care about is God and family. It's hard to explain, but I am a servant (we all are in some shape or form when you think about it). I love to serve, and I love to please. I'm still my own man who knows what he wants, but I also desire to do for others. Jesus took care of himself, but He loved to serve (John 13:1–17). Jesus has no limits, and depending on what I'm doing or who I'm doing it for, I don't either, especially when it's someone I love. So what say you, my love? Will you let me do what I was born to do? To love, cherish, provide, and support you? I'm here for you. All you've got to do is accept it, thank God, and say "I do."

Love to…

A FAMILY

The more I think about it, the more I realize why Jesus was so happy to be around children. I mean, who could not be? Kids, they just want to have fun (and no, I'm not talking about the song). They have no worries in this world, and their trust far exceeds any of us adults. That's another thing God has bestowed upon me. I love my daughter with all my heart and soul. You have an amazing child of your own. She's a princess like no other. My daughter sees her as a sister. Can you see it? Can you see how everything was molded perfectly for us? No, but by the Grace of God's will. It doesn't matter the circumstances; what matters is what we do with them.

Love to...

DESIRE OF THE HEART

When I was in the military, I had an amazing chaplain, very wise, who knew how to preach the Bible. He would always share his testimony, and it always would resonate with me till this day. His testimony was how he became a chaplain. When he met his wife, she said that in order for him to date her, he had to be a Christian. Long story short, he knew she was the one, so he started going to church with her. God changed his heart, and he was called to preach. His testimony taught me something. God can use the desires of one's heart to draw them to Him. Psalm 37:4 ("Delight yourself in the Lord and he will give you the desire of your heart") is a short verse, but it can mean so much. The beauty of it all is that God doesn't ask for much, only that you love him. Wait for me, love. I'm coming.

Love to...

THE TRUTH

Here's the beauty of it all. I don't care if we don't get together, and I say that very lightly because more than anything, I want to be your husband and you, my wife. What's the old saying? It's better to have loved and lost than never to have loved at all. Well, I have loved, and I have lost (maybe), but just because it's lost doesn't mean it's gone. The short time we have had together has been magical. I can still hear your voice in my head, "Why, why do you love me so much?" That's probably the million-dollar question everyone is waiting to hear, right? I'll answer it, but I ask you, why does it matter? Have any of you ever been to a men's or women's group at church or just a group in general? I have, and during my group at church specifically, I mentioned how I desired a wife. I was told to write down everything I wanted my future wife to look and be like. The theory is, nothing is impossible for God (Luke 1:37) because He is the God of creation. Makes sense when you think about it, but it was one of the hardest things I had to do. It was like I could feel God hovering over me, looking at everything I typed. Once I was done, I took a look at it and was like, "Holy cow!" (PG version at least.) I could not believe it. So I shared it with one of the brothers at church and was like, "This can't be right." He mentioned that as you spend more time with God, He's going to change the way to think, and what you wrote down won't be the same. I didn't doubt what he said, but I thought, I've been the same since high school and throughout my time in the service. It would take a miracle. Then I met you, on August 29, 2021, at 5:11 p.m. When I saw you, you laughed, spoke about God, mothered your princess, and were strong for what you wanted. I was blown away. I didn't know what was going on, but I loved every minute. Who is this woman that every time I leave her house, there is an unknown pull that is drawing us together? Who is this woman? After a while, I realized this was nothing mysterious or by chance. This was God changing me right in the midst of us being together. God could have just proven his point and reveal that change, but God did something that no man could ever do. He transformed my eyes so that I would only have eyes for you. Believe me or not! I know what I heard and felt from God. So why isn't she with me, you ask? Well, that's the trillion-dollar question. The answer is quite simple, my friends—free will. God will never force anyone who does not want to be used. I can end this story like this, but I feel as though it is far from over. Don't you?

Love to...

SOMETHING ABOUT THAT NAME

When you have someone who motivates you about God, it is an unknown feeling. But the motivation isn't what you might think; it's actually about your name, my love. There's this song by Kirk Franklin, "Something about That Name." That name that they were singing about was Jesus. Kirk mentions that the name of Jesus sparks a flame when you say, read, or hear His name. It is a breath of life. Listening to the song always had meaning, but after meeting you and falling in love with you, the name Jesus just became personal. Seeing your name every time you text or call, my heart would jump in excitement. I remember that I used to answer the phone so fast when you called. It didn't have time to ring because I was so excited to hear from you. You probably thought that it was something that I set in my phone, but it's not. I never thought it to be a problem because this was new to me. Maybe I should wait to let it ring… (*longest wait of my life!*) The more I think about it, the more I realize that I am not ashamed of my actions, neither am I embarrassed about it. Love stretches as far as the East is from the West. Love can look like so many things, and I have so many things left to show you. So what say you, my love? How far does your love stretch out?

Love to…

LOVE, PRAY, AND DEATH

When you're cooking food or preparing a snack, you always want to make sure that, whatever you are making, the flavors coincide with each other, like peanut butter and jelly. It would be odd if someone said, "I'm going to make peanut butter and ranch." Well, I'm going to be that odd person and talk about death and prayer. Maybe not too odd if you're thinking about a funeral, but with the way I am going to explain it, to most I might just sound a little crazy. Love is a magical word, but most have been through the ringer with that word, like myself. It can be heartbreaking, terrifying, and for those who don't know what it is or feels like, it can have an unknown feeling. So what does that have to do with prayer and death? Ladies and gentlemen, what I'm about to say *does not* have to apply to you, but I have made amends with it, and oddly enough, it has put me at peace. I prayed to my Lord that if my love does not become my wife, I want her to live a longer life than me. Even though she does not want me to be her husband, that doesn't mean my love for her has to end. If it did, then my love for her would be inaccurate and my methodology on love would make me a hypocrite (debatable, I know, but that's where I stand). So take me, Lord. Let her keep living so that she'll know her worth. My love is endless, but wanting to receive it cannot be forced. That doesn't mean mine has to end. No, that just means that I will continue to pray for you while I am in heaven rejoicing.

Love to...

ONLY IN DREAMS

I had another dream. You were there, at the house you always wanted. Five bedrooms, four and a half bathrooms, in a cul-de-sac neighborhood with a big backyard. Honestly, it was magical. You would wake up early in the morning, sit outside on the patio while drinking your coffee. You would look so beautiful wearing one of my shirts, looking up at me saying, "Good morning, baby." I would kiss you as if it were our first time kissing. Kids would run around in the backyard. It's the simple things that make it magical. What do you see when you picture us together in our future home?

Love to...

WHAT IF...

What if we lived in a different world where I would fall in love with you all over again, but when you laid eyes on me, you didn't feel the same way, and you were just taking me for a ride? Do you think my feelings would change? My love for you would not be shaken. What if your heart failed, and you needed a heart, and I had the heart that was a perfect match for you that could save your life? Without hesitation, I would give it up to you. What if I saw a gunman two hundred meters ahead of us and I didn't have time to save the both of us? I would use my body as a shield to protect you. Well, my love, what if...

Love to...

WEDDING

When it comes to weddings, I believe it should be a time not even the heavens could forget. Life's most beautiful combination is spirituality and romance. This is where we witness God joining the man and the woman as one, in a setting that is breathtaking to the audience who is watching the magic happen. The moment that the two become one, when they say, "I do," and kiss. You might not know this, but God takes the two as one, lifts them up on top of the heavens while they kiss, and unites them in communion. Hearts stop as they kiss, only to be born again as one. Reunion never felt so good. How do you see our wedding, my love? Do you see what I see? Do you see it?

Love to...

BASEBALL

My friends, by now you are probably wondering if I am ever going to end up with the love of my life. Well, isn't that life for you, to hit you with so many curveballs, it leaves you at a strike? Until you get a glimpse of where the ball is going to come at you, then you hit it, to get a glimpse of hope or a home run. I'm no baseball pro or an athlete by no means, but I have seen enough games to see how it can relate to our life today. Spoiler alert: I haven't gotten that hit, but if we had players that gave up just because they haven't achieved their goal, there wouldn't be a Yadier Molina. Faith can be a scary and anxious road. It often makes you question who you are as a person, but faith isn't for the weary, and neither is love. But as long as I have strength in my bones, I will continue to give it my all for you.

Love to...

THE SOURCE

I hope by now you see how much God's love can push you, how it has no end to how much you can love someone. The sky is the limit, and it can be so romantic if you just give it a try and don't give up. You can do it. Believe in God, believe that romance can happen through God. Don't be scared, my friends. Too many times we let go what we've been given since birth, but as we grow, that love becomes heavy, overwhelming, and we let it go. Pick it back up, grab onto God's hand again. It only becomes heavy when you don't know where the source came from. My friends, I've given you the answers, but in case you missed it, it's God! God is the source! And it can be amazing, magical, and romantic. I'm a living witness. God has sent me to you, my love.

Love you too

FOOL

Ladies and gentlemen, I want to point out something to you. Any bad situation can be turned right side up for the good. I would laugh when I used to hear people call a woman "PHAT," meaning "pretty, hot, and tempting." Now how about that for turning a situation right side up? I say all that to say, I'm a fool, I'm a big hopeless *fool*! Just for curiosity purposes, I decided to see the possible acronyms for fool, and I have to say not all of them are positive. Most of you are probably familiar with the acronym "FOOL" for "falling out of love." Since this whole book is based on love, I wanted to see how I could turn that bad acronym right side up. I thought to myself, Who am I a fool for, and what am I trying to do? So here it is, my friends, the new and improve acronym for "FOOL" is "figuring out our love." Isn't it what a fool is trying to do to someone who doesn't want to give us a chance? I want you to remember something, my friends: "It takes a smart person to understand your matters, but it takes a fool to understand the matters of your heart." A free quote by yours truly. What do you think, my love? Can you love a fool?

Love to...

TRUTH

Being a "FOOL" is not so bad when you're true to yourself. I'm in love with a woman who doesn't have the same feelings that I have for her. Now some might be thinking, "She doesn't deserve you," or, "There are plenty of woman who would match the love you can offer," or my favorite, "You just need to let her go." My friends, I know all of it. Believe me, my family reminds me of it any chance they get. Here's something else I want you to try to remember: friends, family, church family, or the world would try to give you their opinions based on their experience on love when they see the inevitable in the natural eyes. However, only God has the true say or the last word from where I'm sitting. Sometimes when you want the inevitable or the impossible, you have to go to the source, the one true God that can achieve the impossible. God has still shown me hope, *but* I think the follow-up question now would be, what do you do when God says no? Ha-ha, for that, my friends, you will have to stay tuned. God has still shown me hope. A true Christian does not believe in coincidence; rather, he sees God's work. I know all that I'm saying is argumentative, but when you have a relationship with God, no one, not even you, my love, can say something. Don't get me wrong, this patient and waiting game is the hardest thing that I have ever experienced. Waking up every morning and thinking about you is unreal. All the negative voices in my head are unfathomable. Even if the world turns out to be right about us, I will not stop fighting.

Love to...

YOUR WILL

I'm going to be like Rocky Balboa and tell you something you already know. Forcing, pressuring, or convincing anyone to love you is not going to be the love you deserve. I'm guilty of it. My prayers used to sound like this, "Lord, please let her love me," and, "Please allow her to come to her senses," or, "Lord, let her call me because I don't want to seem pathetic." Ha-ha, you get the point, but I realized, or God made me realize, what good would that do if it is not from the heart? One of my biggest pet peeves is when you see evangelists trying to force someone to their religion or to God. News flash, you can't change anyone's heart or mind. This is why God gave us free will (hint, hint, to the question of what happens when God says no) because coming to the realization on our own or making that step on our own truly means that it was by their own will or from the heart that they made that decision. It kills me when a husband or wife says, "Tell me you love me." Men and women, he or she is only telling you they love you because you told him to say it. He or she is only buying you flowers because you told him to. Your husband or wife is only taking you out because you said to. You get the point: let your husband or wife do or say something special from the heart because they wanted to. Now, if it has been a week or more and your spouse hasn't said or shown you that love you deserve, then, okay, feel free to express your feelings. Feel free to express it anyhow, but I just want you to realize that when your spouse or the person you're in a relationship with openly says, "I love you," it is going to feel so much better to receive it. If I can be so bold to say, I believe that is how God feels when people come to Him. I look forward to the day you come to me and say, "I'm ready."

Love to...

DAYS OF OLD

I saw these old people at the coffee shop. I'm pretty sure they were husband and wife, but whether they were, something about them was so beautiful. They had to be well over eighty years old, but they weren't talking to each other. They were just sitting there next to each other quietly. It's almost as if you could feel their spirits intertwining. I was told that I have a gift of feeling things when it comes to other people. Maybe that is why I felt the love between the two. Normally, I would go up and talk to individuals that I feel I was led to talk to, but for some reason, I already knew what I wanted to know. As I was getting ready to leave, I saw them in the corner of my eye. The man was holding onto his wife (or what I assume to be his wife) and they both were smiling, just content with each other. It made me wonder how we are going to be when we are old. Playful I imagine, even at an old age, but even then, you still would look just as beautiful to me as the first time I laid my eyes on you. If you could imagine us old, how do you see us together? I'm always going to be there for you and take care of you, Lord willing, if you'll let me.

Love to...

MUSIC

Music, I love music. I think we can both agree on our love for music. I'm not a musician and I can't sing, but if I was, I would use it to my advantage and sing and play to you all the days of our lives. You want to know something funny? There is this one song on my playlist that I think about playing when I am with you. It's actually a country song too. I know you've heard it before; it's called, "Chicken Fried" by Zac Brown Band. If you haven't heard it before, I recommend you listen to it. I thank God for music, because when I do not have the right words to say, I know I have someone out there in the world actually singing how I feel. I remember the nights that I couldn't sleep and I would go for a drive, picking people up for Uber. Everybody would always say, "I love your music," or, "Good choice in music," or, "I love your vibe." The list goes on, but honestly, I never thought anything of it because all I was playing was R&B. I told my therapist once that I listen to R&B because it gives me hope in the one true thing that matters in this world, and that's love. What's your song? What's that song on your playlist or radio that anytime it plays, it makes you feel all warm inside because it makes you think of the one you love? What say you, my love, what's your song? Wouldn't it be nice if we could listen to it together? Or perhaps build a new song together.

Love to...

THE SECRET OF THE HEART

Let me tell you a little secret. Have you ever heard from someone, or maybe you have said this before, that the heart is deceitful, that it gets me in trouble, or that it fails? Well, join the club because I am guilty of it, or at least I was. For my Christians out there, that is exactly what the enemy wants you to think. Give me one sentence to preach to you right quick. When you got saved, Jesus gave you a new heart, a new way of thinking. Your heart cannot, will not, go wrong when it is from God. End of sermon. With that being said, we think it goes wrong when we follow our hearts and try to think logically with our mind. There is a reason God says to renew your mind, and I'll leave it there. You can't mix yellow and blue to make red. You're going to be disappointed and wonder why you keep getting green. It takes a smart person to think with their mind, but it takes a wise person to follow their heart. The heart wants what it wants. Don't be afraid of it. It is the source of life. Listen to it. God molded your heart together. If you listen close enough, you get the best of both worlds, your love and God. I wonder what your heart says about me when you think or hear my name. I know what mine says. It says, "Forever."

Love to...

THE JOURNEY

Throughout our journey that led to this very part, I cannot help but think about our future, but that's the thing. The future was just a thought. Neither you nor I could predict what happens in the future or if there will be a future. No one knows but God. There is only the here and now, so what are you going to do with it? If you don't mind, I'm going to share my heart with you, but especially you, my love, and say to you what I would say if I had your hand in marriage. Now I know what you are thinking: Why spoil the moment? Why not wait till you actually have that moment? Well, it is like I said: the future is not promised to us, so why wait? Be encouraged, my friends. Every day is a blessing, and every day is a greater blessing when you have someone to fight for. Enjoy my short poem…

All my life, I have been waiting for someone like you. I didn't know it then like I know it now, that you would be my dream come true. When the world told me no, God told me yes. I wasn't waiting in a straight line, but I did my best, and, in the end, God took care of the rest. There were so many things I had to learn underneath the sun until our time had come, but now we have our entire life together for me to show you the man that I've become. Now here we are with your veil uncovered, with me looking into your beautiful eyes. I want to say I will always love you selflessly and unconditionally with all of my heart, even until death do us part.

Love to, H. H.

THE END

For those of you wondering if I have gotten that woman of my dreams, that woman who encouraged me to even write this message. The answer is no, but not because I was wrong about her or that it was not real. It's just because that desire hasn't reached her heart. It can be a scary thing, which is why we often try to pursue other dreams and desires, ones that cannot hurt us emotionally. Be encouraged, my friends.

One of my favorite verses in the Bible is 1 John 4:7: "There is no fear in love, but perfect love drives out fear, because fear involves punishment, and the one who fears is not perfected in love" (NSAB). Take chances, and as long as it lines up with God's will, then there is no chance you will lose. You might be asking, Well you lost, didn't you? No, my friends, I didn't, because in the beginning it was great, and I know what I felt that day, and it will forever and always be in my heart. Besides, I'm still alive, and God is still in the making, so who knows, maybe her heart will be lifted and I can finally take her hand in marriage. Your story may not end up like mine. You may find that man or woman who is willing and able, no matter the circumstance. Please! God is a God of love. He is love. That's all He knows. If you have read my messages and can relate to some extent (I know for some, it may be to dramatic, ridiculous, or crazy), go after it. I promise it won't fail, because God, who is love, does not fail, so the love that's right in front of you will not fail. Love, my friends, is God's ultimate will for us. Everything else does not matter. I really hope this resides in your heart. I want to leave you with two things:

1. Song of Solomon 8:6–7 (NSAB): "Put me like a seal over your heart, like a seal on your arm. For love is as strong as death,

jealousy is as severe as Sheol; its flames are flames of fire, the flame of the Lord. Many waters cannot quench love, nor will rivers flood over it; if a man were to give all the riches of his house for love, it would be utterly despised."

Look at this! For love is as strong as death! Many waters cannot quench love, nor will rivers flood over! My friends, do you see how powerful and beautiful that is? In a nutshell, nothing can stop love.

Lastly, I will follow up with this, and please do not think I am trying to take away the primary context for the verses, but if we cannot apply what God has given us, then we take away the power that His word gives.

2. Hosea 1:2; 2:7; 3:3: When the Lord first spoke through Hosea, the Lord said to Hosea, "Go, take for yourself a wife inclined to infidelity, and children of infidelity; for the land commits flagrant infidelity, abandoning the Lord". And she will pursue her lovers, but she will not reach them; and she will seek them but will not find them. Then she will say, "I will go back to my first husband, because it was better for me then than now!" Then I said to her, "You shall live with me for many days. You shall not play the prostitute, nor shall you have *another* man; so I will also be toward you."

Again, I am not trying to take away the context or the primary meaning behind the verses because the book of Hosea is primarily about God's sacrificial love for Israel. Israel is metaphorically Gomer, and God is metaphorically Hosea. This story to me is the most romantic love story in the Bible, but let's apply it to us. We see in chapter 1, verse 2, that God wants Hosea to be with a woman who is not right for him. Then, in chapter 2, verse 7, the woman he wants to be with does not want to be with him. (Sounds like something I said earlier about my love, doesn't it? It just gets better.) Then God changes her heart and brings Gomer back to Hosea (hmm, God is the same yesterday, today, and forever (Hebrew 13:8). I told you my friends, God is still in the making). Lastly, in chapter 3, verse 3, Hosea fights for back and kindles an even more powerful love than before.

There you have it, my friends. I really hope you enjoyed this reading. I know I got something out of it: a new hope that I can add to my arsenal. Please, I'm not telling you what to believe in; I'm just telling you what matters most in this world. If you have love, what's there left to want in this lifetime until we get to the Kingdom of God? The beauty of it all is that the love that you store on Earth will never die, because God lives forever. Be blessed, my friends.

Love to...

The world began with love, and it is going to end with love. Who do you want to start and end your love with? Add your love's initials and start your journey. It doesn't matter whether he or she feels the same. Love spreads out, and if God didn't have that mindset, the body of Christ would be very small.

Milton Keynes UK
Ingram Content Group UK Ltd.
UKHW021911231124
451423UK00006B/676

9 798822 958920